Laughing Time

Laughing Time

Nonsense Poems

William Jay Smith

Illustrated
by
Fernando
Krahn

A Merloyd Lawrence Book
DELACORTE PRESS/SEYMOUR LAWRENCE

A MERLOYD LAWRENCE BOOK
Published by
Delacorte Press/Seymour Lawrence
1 Dag Hammarskjold Plaza
New York, N.Y. 10017

Some of the poems in this collection first appeared in the following
books by William Jay Smith: LAUGHING TIME, BOY BLUE'S
BOOK OF BEASTS, PUPTENTS AND PEBBLES, MR. SMITH
AND OTHER NONSENSE, and also in *Cricket Magazine*.

Manufactured in the United States of America

First printing

Designed by Terry Antonicelli

Library of Congress Cataloging in Publication Data

Smith, William Jay, 1918–
    Laughing time.

    "A Merloyd Lawrence book."
    SUMMARY: Contains nonsense poems on a variety of topics.
    1. Nonsense verses, American. [1. Nonsense verses.
2. American poetry.] I. Krahn, Fernando. II. Title.
PS3537.M8693L3   811'.54   80-65839
ISBN 0-440-05534-2
ISBN 0-440-05535-0 (lib. bdg).

To
my granddaughter,
Marissa Jeanne

CONTENTS

THE OLD MAN FROM OKEFENOKEE:

THE FLOOR AND THE CEILING

The King of Hearts

"I like this book," said the King of Hearts.
"It makes me laugh the way it starts!"

"I like it also!" said his Mother.
So they sat down and read it to each other.

LAUGHING TIME

Laughing Time

It was laughing time, and the tall Giraffe
Lifted his head, and began to laugh:

Ha! Ha!   Ha! Ha!

And the Chimpanzee on the ginkgo tree
Swung merrily down with a *Tee Hee Hee:*

Hee! Hee!   Hee! Hee!

"It's certainly not against the law!"
Croaked Justice Crow with a loud guffaw:

Haw! Haw!   Haw! Haw!

The dancing Bear who could never say "No"
Waltzed up and down on the tip of his toe:

Ho! Ho!   Ho! Ho!

The Donkey daintily took his paw,
And around they went: Hee-Haw! Hee-Haw!

Hee-Haw!   Hee-Haw!

The Moon had to smile as it started to climb;
All over the world it was laughing time!

Ho! Ho!   Ho! Ho!   Hee-Haw!   Hee-Haw!
Hee! Hee!   Hee! Hee!   Ha! Ha!   Ha! Ha!

Why

Why do apricots look like eggs?
> Why?

Why do sofas have four legs?
> Why?

Why do buses stop and go?
Why do roosters strut and crow?
Why do bugles blow and blow?
Why is Sunday? I don't know
> Why!

The Land of Ho-Ho-Hum

When you want to go wherever you please,
Just sit down in an old valise,
    And fasten the strap
    Around your lap,
And fly off over the apple trees.

And fly for days and days and days
Over rivers, brooks, and bays
    Until you come
    To Ho-Ho-Hum,
Where the Lion roars, and the Donkey brays.

Where the Unicorn's tied to a golden chain,
And Umbrella Flowers drink the rain.
    After that,
    Put on your hat,
Then sit down and fly home again.

Hats

Round or square
Or tall or flat,
People love
To wear a hat.

Around My Room

I put on a pair of overshoes
And walk around my room,
With my Father's bamboo walking stick,
And my Mother's feather broom.

I walk and walk and walk and walk,
I walk and walk around.
I love my Father's tap-tap-tap,
My Mother's feathery sound.

Jack-in-the-Box

A Jack-in-the-Box
On the pantry shelf
Fell in the coffee
And hurt himself.
Nobody looked
To see what had happened:
There by the steaming
Hot urn he lay;
So they picked him up
With the silverware
And carried him off
On the breakfast tray.

Over and Under

Bridges are for going over water,
Boats are for going over sea;
Dots are for going over dotted *i*'s,
And blankets are for going over me.

    Over and under,
        Over and under,
            Crack the whip,
                And hear the thunder.

Divers are for going under water,
Seals are for going under sea;
Fish are for going under mermaids' eyes,
And pillows are for going under me.

    Over and under,
        Over and under,
            Crack the whip,
                And hear the thunder,
                    Crack-crack-crack,
                        Hear the crack of thunder!

Apples

Some people say that apples are red,
And some people say they're blue.
Here is a blue one for that little boy,
And here is a red one for you.

The Mirror

I look in the Mirror, and what do I see?
A little of you, and a lot of me!

Spilt Milk: Whodunit

Whodunit?
  Who?

"I," said the Crow,
"If you really want to know."

Whodunit?
  Who?

"I," said the Deer,
Grinning ear to ear.

Whodunit?
  Who?

"I," said the Cockatoo,
"Didn't you want me to?"

Whodunit?
  Who?

"I," said the Bear,
"I did it on a dare."

Whodunit?
  Who?

"I," said the Stoat,
Rowing off in a boat.

Whodunit?
  Who?

"I," said the Fox,
From under the box.

Whodunit?
Who?

Up the Hill

Hippety-Hop, goes the Kangaroo,
And the big brown Owl goes, Hoo-Hoo-Hoo!
Hoo-Hoo-Hoo and Hippety-Hop,
Up the Hill, and over the Top!

Baa-Baa-Baa, goes the little white Lamb,
And the Gate that is stuck goes, Jim-Jam-Jam!
Jim-Jam-Jam and Baa-Baa-Baa,
Here we go down again, Tra-La-La!

The Toaster

A silver-scaled Dragon with jaws flaming red
Sits at my elbow and toasts my bread.
I hand him fat slices, and then, one by one,
He hands them back when he sees they are done.

Moon

I have a white cat whose name is Moon;
He eats catfish from a wooden spoon,
And sleeps till five each afternoon.

Moon goes out when the moon is bright
And sycamore trees are spotted white
To sit and stare in the dead of night.

Beyond still water cries a loon,
Through mulberry leaves peers a wild baboon,
And in Moon's eyes I see the moon.

Mrs. Caribou

Old Mrs. Caribou lives by a lake
In the heart of darkest Make-Believe;
She rides through the air on a rickety rake,
And feeds crawfish to a twitchety snake
That sleeps in a basket of African weave.
She sits by the fire when the lights are out
And eats toadstools and sauerkraut,
And bowls of thick white milkweed stew.
If you knock at her door, she will rise and shout,
"Away with you, you roustabout!
My cupboard is bare, my fire is out,
And my door is closed to the likes of you!
Go tie yourself to a hickory stake,
Put a stone on your neck, and jump in the lake.
                AWAY!"

When the fire burns low and the lights are out
And the moon climbs high above the lake,
And the shutters bang, and the ceilings quake,
Mrs. Caribou comes on her rickety rake
And tries to turn you inside out.
But when she does, what you can do
Is snap your fingers and cry, "Shoo!
Away with YOU, Mrs. Caribou!"
Then she will fly back to Make-Believe
With her snake in a basket of African weave,
And finish her bowl of milkweed stew;

And NEVER come back to bother you.
Shoo, Mrs. Caribou! Shoo, Mrs. Caribou!

Shoo, Mrs. Caribou!

Shoo!

Shoo!

SHOO!

Alice

There once was a fat little pig named Alice
    Who hated the things that money can buy.
    She wallowed happily in her sty,
While they ate ice cream in the Royal Palace.

Dictionary

A Dictionary's where you can look things up
 To see if they're really there:
  To see if what you breathe is AIR,
  If what you sit on is a CHAIR,
  If what you comb is curly HAIR,
  If what you drink from is a CUP.
A Dictionary's where you can look things up
 To see if they're really there.

When Candy Was Chocolate

When candy was chocolate and bread was white,
When the yellow pencil began to write,
And the hippopotamus said, "Good night!"
My little sister turned out the light.

Then round and round and round in the dark
I dreamt that I sailed on Noah's ark
Past the big blue whale and the hammerhead shark
Round and round and round in the dark.

Round and round until it was light
And beyond the window was land in sight,
Candy was chocolate, bread was white,
And the yellow pencil began to write.

Big and Little

Big boys do,
    Little boys don't.

Big boys will,
    Little boys won't.

Big boys can,
    Little boys can't.

Big boys shall,
    Little boys shan't.

But when little boys
    Are as big as YOU,

Then turn it around
    And it's just as true:

Big boys *don't*,
    Little boys *do*.

Jittery Jim

There's room in the bus
For the two of us,
But not for Jittery Jim.

He has a train
And a rocket plane,
He has a seal
That can bark and swim,
And a centipede
With wiggly legs,
And an ostrich
Sitting on ostrich eggs,
And crawfish
Floating in oily kegs!

There's room in the bus
For the two of us,
But we'll shut the door on *him!*

Molly Mock-Turtle

Molly Mock-Turtle of Ocean View
Was stirring a kettle of lobster stew
When she heard in the cupboard a terrible din
As of Kangaroos boxing on roofs of tin,
Or Blue Jays conversing in mandarin.
She put out her hand for the rolling pin,
Lost her balance, and fell in the stew.
They found her there in Ocean View
Cooked pink as a lobster up to her chin.

Love

I love you, I like you,
I really do like you.
I do *not* want to strike you,
I do *not* want to shove you.
I *do* want to like you,
I *do* want to love you;
And like you and love you
And love you and love you.

My Body

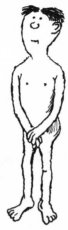

Wherever I go, it also goes,
And when it's dressed, I'm wearing clothes.

Betsy Robin

Betsy Robin packs her bags,
Picks up all that she can carry,
Then flies away to Kingdom Come
Beyond the tip of Tipperary.

Come back, Betsy, come back home!
We miss you more than anything.
It's always winter when you're gone;
Come back, Betsy, and it's spring!

Pick Me Up

Pick me up with a pile of blocks
And carry me past the Cuckoo Clocks!

Pick me up with a pile of hay
And carry me off to Buzzards Bay!

Pick me up with a pile of snow
And carry me out to Idaho!

Pick me up with a pile of twine
And carry me down to the Argentine!

Pick me up with a pile of lava
And carry me over the hills of Java!

Pick me up with a pile of sand
And put me down in Newfoundland!

The Queen of the Nile

Said the Queen of the Nile
By the green palm tree:
"It is our desire
That you come to tea
Thursday at twenty-three
Past three
Under the Royal Canopy
In Our Golden Barge
On the River Nile
Beside the Mediterranean
Sea."

I bowed, and said:
"Most certainly!"
To the Queen of the Nile
By the green palm tree.

Fish

Look at the fish!
Look at the fish!

Look at the fish that is blue and green,
Look at the fish that is tangerine!
Look at the fish that is gold and black
With monocled eye and big humpback!
Look at the fish with the ring in his nose,
And a mouth he cannot open or close!
Look at the fish with lavender stripes
And long front teeth like organ pipes,
And fins that are finer than Irish lace.
Look at that funny grin on his face,
Look at him swimming all over the place!

Look at the fish!
Look at the fish!
Look at the fish!
They're so *beautiful!*

Mistress Mary

Mistress Mary, quite contrary,
What can you carry?

Can you carry
A flowerpot?
A platter
Steaming hot?
A blotter
With a blot?
A rope
Tied in a knot?
A lizard
From a grot?
A top-heavy
Whatnot?
A canvas
Army cot?
A leopard cub
Called Spot?
A happy
Hottentot?

Mistress Mary, quite contrary,
You can carry
An *awful* lot!

People

Hour after hour,
In many places,
People sit,
Making faces.

Having

A castle has
       a castle moat,
A river has
       a river boat,
An organ has
       an organ note,
A mountain has
       a mountain goat,
But look at my
       new overcoat!

The Panda

A lady who lived in Uganda
Was outrageously fond of her Panda:
    With her Chinchilla Cat,
    It ate grasshopper fat
On an air-conditioned veranda.

The Owl

The Owl that lives in the old oak tree
Opens his eyes and cannot see
When it's clear as day to you and me;
But not long after the sun goes down
And the Church Clock strikes in Tarrytown
And Nora puts on her green nightgown,
He opens his big bespectacled eyes
And shuffles out of the hollow tree,
And flies and flies
                and flies and flies,
And flies and flies
                and flies and flies.

Grandmother Ostrich

Grandmother Ostrich goes to bed
With a towel wrapped around her head;
And even if it's bright as day,
She carries a candle to light her way.

Grandmother Ostrich crosses the sand
To the edge of Never-Never Land;
She looks all about her and sees not a soul,
Then pokes her head in an ostrich hole.

Things

Trains are for going,
Boats are for rowing,
Seeds are for sowing,
Noses for blowing,
    And sleeping's for bed.

Dogs are for pawing,
Logs are for sawing,
Crows are for cawing,
Rivers for thawing,
    And sleeping's for bed.

Flags are for flying,
Stores are for buying,
Glasses for spying,
Babies for crying,
    And sleeping's for bed.

Cows are for mooing,
Chickens for shooing,
Blue is for bluing,
Things are for doing,
    And sleeping's for bed.

Games are for playing,
Hay is for haying,
Horses for neighing,
Saying's for saying,
    And sleeping's for bed.

Money's for spending,
Patients for tending,
Branches for bending,
Poems for ending,
    And sleeping's for bed.

PUPTENTS
AND PEBBLES:
A Nonsense ABC

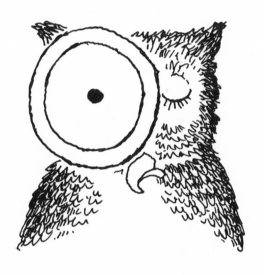

"Puptents and Pebbles,"
　　Said the King to the Queen;
"The words go together,
　　But what do they mean?"

"They make no more sense,"
　　Said the Queen with a grin,
"Than a hairbrush of feathers
　　Or toothbrush of tin."

The King burst out laughing,
　　The Prince came to see;
Then they all read the letters—

A　　　　**B**　　　　**C**　　　　**D**

A is for ALPACA

A small woolly llama;
At night to his Mummy
The Alpaca says: "Mama,
Tuck me into my bed
In my woolly pyjama!"

a is for alpaca

B is for BATS

At night when the Bats
In their mouse-colored capes
And crumpled-up hats
Fly in through the door,
People scream: "Look out—BATS!"

b is for bats

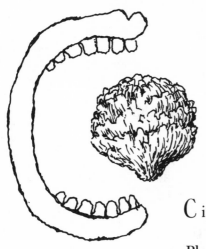

C is for CABBAGES

Planted in rows,
Each has a green head
But no fingers or toes,
No arms and no legs,
No eyes and no nose.

c is for cabbages

D is for DOG

Says the prancing French poodle
As he trots with the band
When it plays "Yankee Doodle":
"Bow-wow! I hate CATS—
The whole kit-and-caboodle!"

d is for dog

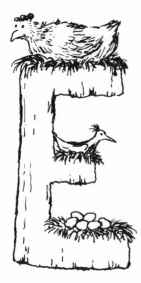

E is for EGG

Which the chicken has laid.
From the newly laid Egg
A chicken is made;
By the newly made chicken
A new Egg is laid.

e is for egg

F is for FROG-BOY

Frog-boy dives in
With mask and frog-flippers
Where parrot fish grin;
And brings up a squid
In an old sardine tin.

f is for frog-boy

G is for GOAT

An old Billy Goat
Sang hillbilly songs
As he rowed in a boat;
A fish yanked his beard,
And he hit a high note!

g is for goat

H is for HAT

Green, yellow, or red,
Stovepipe or turban,
It sits on your head;
Remove it when bathing
Or when going to bed.

h is for hat

I is for INKSPOT

A spot of black ink
Looks to you like a yak,
Looks to me like a mink;
An Inkspot can look
Like whatever you think.

i is for inkspot

J is for JACK-IN-THE-BOX

Flip open the box;
And, a cat from a bag,
Jack *jumps* from the box
With a long paper neck
And no shoes or socks.

j is for jack-in-the-box

K is for KING

He says, with a frown,
"My cocoa is cold,
You contemptible clown;
And this upside-down cake
Is NOT upside down!"

k is for king

L is for LAUNDRY

The clothes that get clean
In a washtub or basin
Or washing machine;
Then again they get dirty,
And again they get clean.

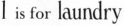

l is for laundry

M is for MASK

It changes a lot
To add a new face
To the face you have got;
Then the person you are
Is the person you're not.

m is for mask

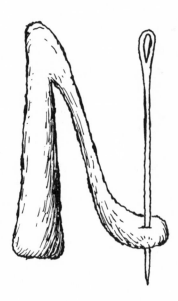

N is for NEEDLE

It squinted and said,
"I have only one eye!"
"I have none," said the thread.
"Lend me yours, and we'll sew!"
So they sewed—so they said.

n is for needle

O is for OWL

The Owl, it is said,
Has eyes he can't move
Without moving his head;
So he lets out a hoot
And stares straight ahead.

O is for owl

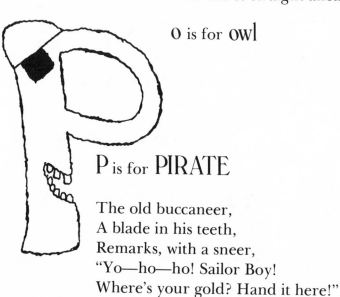

P is for PIRATE

The old buccaneer,
A blade in his teeth,
Remarks, with a sneer,
"Yo—ho—ho! Sailor Boy!
Where's your gold? Hand it here!"

p is for pirate

Q is for QUEEN

The Mad Queen in red
Cries, "Button your raincoat!
Off with your head!"
And they say to her, "Ma'am,
Do you *know* what you've said?"

q is for queen

R is for REINDEER

In Lapland the Lapps
Drive teams of Reindeer
On the frozen icecaps,
With Reindeer lap rugs
Pulled over their laps.

r is for reindeer

S is for SPRINGS

On the Springs in a chair
You wobble, you bounce.
You are here, you are there—
Then, up to no good,
You fly through the air.

S is for springs

T is for TUB

In a Tub one fine day
A pig and a parrot
Went paddling away;
They steered with a clothespin,
And sang *Oink! Olé!*

t is for tub

U is for UP

High Up on the ceiling
I see a house fly.
What can he be feeling
Looking down at his floor
When his floor is the ceiling?

u is for up

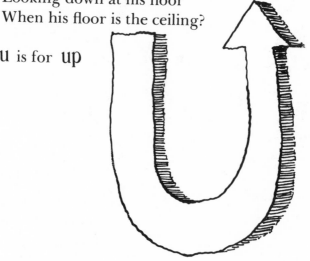

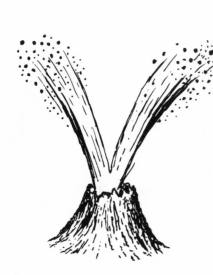

V is for VOLCANO

A bright mountaintop;
It rumbles and grumbles
Until it can't stop.
With hot rock and ashes
It then blows its top.

V is for volcano

W is for WELL

In the Well is Well water,
And into the Well
Fell the Well-digger's daughter.
Her brother he saved her—
By one foot he caught her!

W is for well

X is for X

And X marks the spot
On the rug in the parlor,
The sand in the lot,
Where once you were standing,
And now you are not.

X is for X

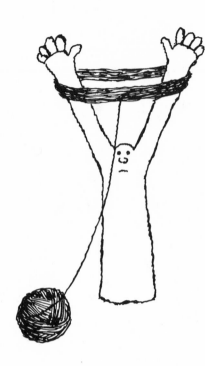

Y is for YARN

The wool that's unwound
From the ball by the cat
Who bats it around;
And gets it wound up
So it can't be unwound.

y is for yarn

Z is for ZEBU

Says the humpbacked Zebu,
"Well, trim my haystack!
Look at me—look at you!
Look again at the letters,
And say them all through!

Zip-Zip! Zingaroo!
Off your sock!
Off your shoe!
Off to BED now with
YOU!"

z is for zebu

"Puptents and Pebbles,"
    Said the King to the Queen;
"The words went together,
    But what did they mean?"

"They made no more sense,"
    Said the Queen to the King,
"Than a pet lobster led
    Through the street on a string!"

The Prince laughed and laughed
    Till he nodded his head,
And took the book with him
    Upstairs to bed.

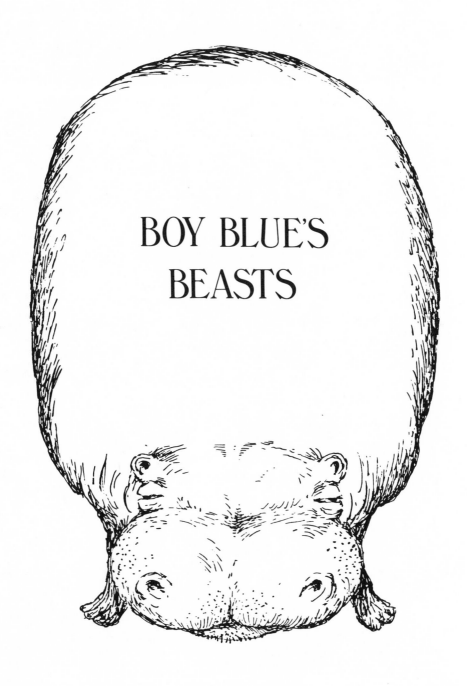

BOY BLUE'S
BEASTS

Elephant

When you put me up on the Elephant's back,
I'll go round the world and never come back.
I will travel for miles away from home
To London, Paris, Vienna, Rome;
I will journey to India and Siam,
And when people ask me who I am,
I'll say to them all: "My name is Boy Blue.
This is my Elephant; who are you?"
I will ask them all if they'd like to see
The Beasts in my menagerie;
Then if they would, I will show them through
The whole of the world and the whole of the zoo.

Monkey

High on a banyan tree in a row
Sat three black Monkeys when it started to snow.
The first Monkey lifted his paw and said:
"I think I must have a cold in the head;
Though snow in a jungle just cannot be,
That certainly looks like snow to me."
The second exclaimed: "I would also
Be inclined to say that it was snow;
But there may be something wrong with me."
Third Monkey—wisest of the three—
Cried, "Look!" and pointed high in the tree.
A fourth Monkey stood there shaking a vine
Heavy with blossoms white and fine
Which fell through the air like flakes of snow
On the upturned faces there below—
And continued to fall till the jungle green
Was changed into a winter scene,
And huge white petals without sound
Had swept in drifts across the ground.

Tiger

A hunter cried out when he spotted a Tiger,
"What a beautiful rug that creature would make!"
The Tiger growled: he did not agree;
He chased the hunter up a tree.
The hunter's gun went Bang! Bang! Bang!
Zing! Zing! Zing! the bullets sang;
A bunch of bananas plopped to the ground.
The Tiger laughed as he danced around.
He laughed so very hard, poor fellow,
Off flew his stripes of black and yellow.

When lightning flashes through the sky
And the candle glows in my cat's eye;
When thunder rolls from organ pipes,
I think I see those Tiger stripes,
I think I see them whizzing by
In streaks of lightning through the sky.

Yak

The long-haired Yak has long black hair,
He lets it grow—he doesn't care.
He lets it grow and grow and grow,
He lets it trail along the stair.
Does he ever go to the barbershop? NO!
How wild and woolly and devil-may-care
A long-haired Yak with long black hair
Would look when perched in a barber chair!

Parrot (from Trinidad)

I bought me a Parrot in Trinidad
   And all the Parrot could say
When it got really good and mad,
Was something that sounded terribly bad:

> *Lolloping Lumberjack! Old Baghdad!*
> *Cold Kamchatka! Hot heat pad!*

But then, when it felt gay,
The Parrot I bought in Trinidad
Would cry with all the voice that it had:

> *Lovely Lollipop! Pink Doodad!*
> *Sweet Elephants!*
> *Hooray!*

Antelope

When he takes a bath, the Antelope
Uses lots of water and little soap;
Then he shakes himself dry and runs up the slope
As clean as a whistle—or so I hope.

Up the bank quickly the Antelope goes
And on the tall grass he rubs his wet nose.
Down from his ears the cool water flows;
He runs up the bank—and away he goes!

Pig

Pigs are always awfully dirty;
    I do not think it bothers me.
If I were a Pig, I would say: "My dears,
I do not intend to wash my ears
Once in the next eleven years,
    No matter how dirty they may be!"

Pigs are always awfully muddy;
    I do not think I really care.
If I were a Pig, I would say: "My honeys,
While you stay as clean as the Easter bunnies,
I'll curl in the mud and read the funnies,
    And never, never comb my hair!"

Lion

The Beast that is most fully dressed
Is the Lion in the yellow vest,
The velvet robes of royal red,
A crown of diamonds on his head.
His mane is combed, his paws are clean,
He looks most kingly and serene.
He rises from his royal throne
Beside his golden telephone,
And paces up and down the floor;
He groans, he growls, he starts to roar,
He roars again, he growls some more,
He tears apart his yellow vest,
He takes his robes, his diamond crown,
His telephone, and throws them down,
He kicks them all around the floor.
He gets in such a frightful rage
They have to lock him in a cage
Until he slowly quiets down
And they can give him back his crown,
His velvet robes, his yellow vest,
And he is once more fully dressed.

Camel

The Camel is a long-legged humpbacked beast
With the crumpled-up look of an old worn shoe.
He walks with a creep and a slouch and a slump
As over the desert he carries his hump
Like a top-heavy ship, like a bumper bump-bump.
See him plodding in caravans out of the East,
Bringing silk for a party and dates for a feast.
Is he tired? Is he *thirsty?* No, not in the least.
Good morning, Sir Camel! Good morning to you!

Seal

See how he dives
  From the rocks with a zoom!
See how he darts
    Through his watery room
    Past crabs and eels
    And green seaweed,
    Past fluffs of sandy
    Minnow feed!
  See how he swims
    With a swerve and a twist,
  A flip of the flipper,
  A flick of the wrist!
  Quicksilver-quick,
  Softer than spray,
  Down he plunges
And sweeps away;
Before you can think,
Before you can utter
Words like "Dill pickle"
Or "Apple butter,"
  Back up he swims
  Past Sting Ray and Shark,
  Out with a zoom,
  A whoop, a bark;
    Before you can say
    Whatever you wish,
    He plops at your side
    With a mouthful of fish!

Dragon

A Dragon named Ernest Belflour,
Who lived in a dark palace tower,
    Played an old violin
    Of dried-out sharkskin
Hour after hour after hour.

An Indian Princess one day,
Who happened to wander that way,
    Said: "The sound of that thin
    Dried-out violin
Has stolen my heart away."

So she climbed the steps of the tower
And there beheld Ernest Belflour,
    Who was changed by her glance
    To a handsome young Prince:
She had broken the Old Witch's power.

They were married the very next minute
By a neighbor, Sir Larchmont of Linnet,
    And they danced to a thin
    Dried-out violin
Accompanied by a very shrill spinet.

And Ernest said: "Princess, my dear,
I will never blow smoke in your ear,
    No Dragon am I
    But a Prince till I die;
You have nothing whatever to fear.

"Let me buy you some angelfood cake
That we'll munch while we walk by the lake,
    Enjoying the smile
    Of the sweet Crocodile,
And the music the Bullfrogs make.

"When a Dragon roars down from the hill,
Having come to do us both ill,
    Belching up flames
    And calling us names,
I will say, 'GO AWAY!' And he will."

Whale

When I swam underwater I saw a Blue Whale
Sharing the fish from his dinner pail,
    In an undersea park
    With two Turtles, a Shark,
An Eel, a Squid, and a giant Snail.

When dinner was over, I saw the Blue Whale
Pick up his guests in his dinner pail,
    And swim through the park
    With two Turtles, a Shark,
An Eel, a Squid, and a giant Snail.

Opossum

Have you ever in your life seen a Possum play
    possum?
Have you ever in your life seen a Possum play
    dead?
When a Possum is trapped and can't get away
He turns up his toes and lays down his head,
Bats both his eyes and rolls over dead.
But then when you leave him and run off to play,
The Possum that really was just playing possum
Gets up in a flash and scurries away.

Kangaroo

A tough Kangaroo named Hopalong Brown
Boxed all the badmen out of town.
When he came hopping back home one day,
They presented him with a big bouquet
And named him the Champion of Animal Town.
Hip, Hip, Hooray for Hopalong Brown!

Three cheers for the Champion, Hopalong Brown!
(All of you badmen, get out of town!)
Three cheers for his wife, Mrs. Hopalong Crockett,
And the Hopalong kiddies tucked in her pocket!
Long may he wear his Tumbleweed Crown,
Three cheers for the Champion, Hopalong Brown!

Hip
   Hip
      Hooray!
Hip Hip
     Hooray!
Hip   Hip
    HOORAY!

Unicorn

The Unicorn with the long white horn
   Is beautiful and wild.
He gallops across the forest green
So quickly that he's seldom seen
Where Peacocks their blue feathers preen
   And strawberries grow wild.
He flees the hunter and the hounds,
Upon black earth his white hoof pounds,
Over cold mountain streams he bounds
   And comes to a meadow mild;
There, when he kneels to take his nap,
He lays his head in a lady's lap
   As gently as a child.

Hen

The little red Hen does not write with a pen,
She uses her feet to scratch in the clay.
To me the hen-scratching looks like Greek
Or Turkish, which I cannot speak.
What on earth is she trying to say?

Is she trying to say that the leaves are turning,
The sky is falling, the toast is burning,
That worms have got into her chicken feed?
Around her, yellow fluffs of sun,
The little chickens chirp and run,
And whatever she writes, they rush to read.

Anteater

The Anteater makes a meal of ants
That run up and down the leaves of plants.
No matter how hungry *I* ever got,
I wouldn't eat *Ants,* I would certainly not.
I think that Ants would make me squirm;
I'd rather eat an angleworm;
Or if it really came to that,
A mashed mosquito or a gnat,
But not a big red twitchety ant
That crawls on a fat green tropical plant.

Mole

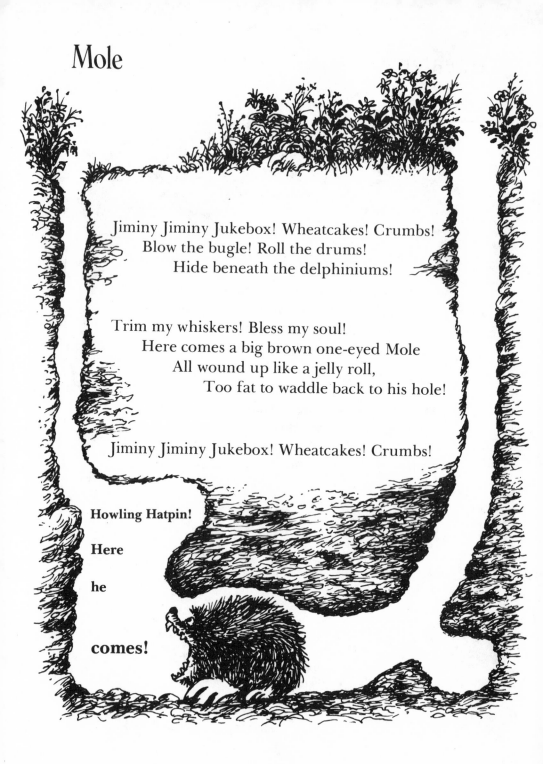

Jiminy Jiminy Jukebox! Wheatcakes! Crumbs!
Blow the bugle! Roll the drums!
Hide beneath the delphiniums!

Trim my whiskers! Bless my soul!
Here comes a big brown one-eyed Mole
All wound up like a jelly roll,
Too fat to waddle back to his hole!

Jiminy Jiminy Jukebox! Wheatcakes! Crumbs!

Howling Hatpin!

Here

he

comes!

Rhinoceros

You may hang your hat on the nose of the Rhino—
    There's really no better place for your hat—
But leave your overcoat in the closet,
    And wipe your feet on the front-door mat.

You may hang your hat on the nose of the Rhino,
    That's what the Rhino's nose is for;
But do not whoop when you cross the hallway
    And troop like Indians through the door.

Don't dance along the warpath, grunting, swaying,
    In the jungle you have found beneath
        those chairs,
Or the Rhino may forget you're only playing,
    And *charge*—and chase you all downstairs.

Coati-Mundi

As I went walking one fine Sunday,
I happened to meet a Coati-Mundi.
    "Coati-Mundi," I said,
    "It's a lovely Sunday
As sure as you're a Coati-Mundi,
A handsome long-tailed Coati-Mundi
    With eyes peering out,
    A flexible snout,
And a raccoon coat all furry and bundly!"

"I quite agree," said the Coati-Mundi,
"It is indeed a most beautiful Sunday.
    What joy for the eye!
    What clouds! What sky!
    What fields of rye!
    Oh, never have I
In all my life seen such a Sunday!"

So he took my hand, and we walked together,
I and my friend, the Coati-Mundi,
Enjoying that most unusual weather,
Enjoying that most delightful Sunday.

Zebra

Are Zebras black with broad white stripes,
Or are they really white with black?
Answer me that and I'll give you some candy
And a green-and-yellow jumping jack.

The finest animal I know
Is the good black Water Buffalo.
    When the sun of the East beats down on the clay
    And coconuts fall and palm trees sway,
    He plods through the rice field day after day.
With graceful long horns, he is gentle and slow:
    I love the Water Buffalo!

Goony Bird

The silliest fowl, the most absurd,
Is certainly the Goony Bird.
When a Goony tumbles to the ground
All he will do is flop around,
Roll his dumbbell eyes and stare
Off into the empty air.
Of silly fowl I know another—
The Booby Bird, the Goony's brother.
The Dodo, too, that's found no more
In Mozambique or Singapore.
Dead is the Dodo, gone is the Auk
That couldn't fly but only walk.
Goony Bird, Booby Bird, Dodo, Auk,
Don't let me hear that silly talk—
Come on, Goony, get up and try
To flap your clumsy wings and fly!

Butterfly

Of living creatures most I prize
Black-spotted yellow Butterflies
Sailing softly through the skies,

Whisking light from each sunbeam,
Gliding over field and stream—
Like fans unfolding in a dream,

Like fans of gold lace flickering
Before a drowsy elfin king
For whom the thrush and linnet sing—

Soft and beautiful and bright
As hands that move to touch the light
When Mother leans to say good night.

Crocodile

The Crocodile wept bitter tears,
    And when I asked him why,
He said: "I weep because the years
    Go far too quickly by!

"I weep because of oranges,
    I weep because of pears,
Because of broken door hinges,
    And dark and crooked stairs.

"I weep because of black shoestrings,
    I weep because of socks,
I weep because I can't do things
    Like dance and shadowbox.

"I weep because the deep blue sea
    Washes the sand in a pile;
I weep because, as you can see,
    I've never learned to smile!"

"To weep like that cannot be fun,
    My reptile friend," I said;
"Your nose, though long, will run and run,
    Your eyes, though wide, be red.

"Why must you so give way to grief?
    You *could* smile if you chose;
Here, take this pocket handkerchief
    And wipe your eyes and nose.

"Come, laugh because of oranges,
    And laugh because of pears,

Because of broken door hinges,
    And dark and crooked stairs.

"Come, laugh because of black shoestrings,
    And laugh because of socks,
And laugh because you *can* do things
    Like dance and shadowbox.

"Come, laugh because it feels so good—
    It's not against the law.
Throw open, as a reptile should,
    Your green and shining jaw!"

The Crocodile he thought awhile
    Till things seemed not so black;
He smiled, and I returned his smile,
    He smiled, and I smiled back.

He took an orange and a pear;
    He took shoestrings and socks,
And tossing them into the air,
    Began to waltz and box.

The animals came, and they were gay:
    The Bobcat danced with the Owl;
The Bat brought tea on a bamboo tray
    To the Yak and Guinea Fowl.

The Monkeys frolicked in the street;
    The Lion, with a smile,
Came proudly down the steps to greet
    The happy Crocodile!

Tapir

How odd it would be if ever a Tapir,
Wrapped in gold and silver paper
And tied with a bow in the shape of a T,
Sat there in the corner beside the tree
When I tiptoed down at six in the morning—
A Christmas present from you to me!

Into the town then we would caper,
I and the ugly, pink-nosed Tapir,
And people would gather round to see.
They would publish our picture in the paper,
And, with it, the words:

BOY BLUE AND THE TAPIR
THAT HE FOUND BENEATH
HIS CHRISTMAS TREE

Hippopotamus

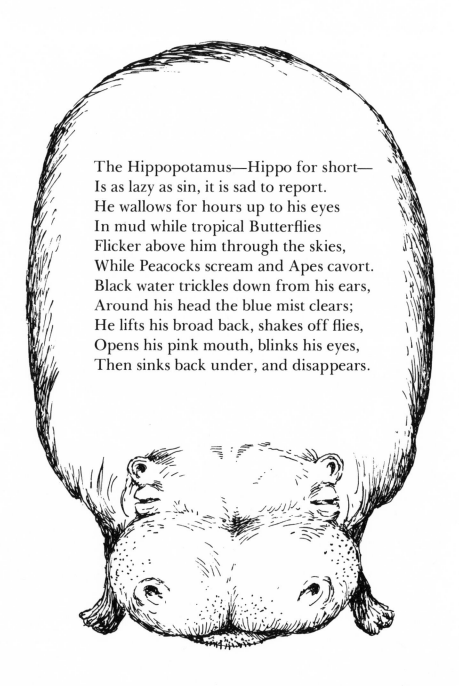

The Hippopotamus—Hippo for short—
Is as lazy as sin, it is sad to report.
He wallows for hours up to his eyes
In mud while tropical Butterflies
Flicker above him through the skies,
While Peacocks scream and Apes cavort.
Black water trickles down from his ears,
Around his head the blue mist clears;
He lifts his broad back, shakes off flies,
Opens his pink mouth, blinks his eyes,
Then sinks back under, and disappears.

Cat

Cats are not at all like people,
     Cats are Cats.

People wear stockings and sweaters,
Overcoats, mufflers, and hats.
Cats wear nothing: they lie by the fire
For twenty-four hours if they desire.
They do NOT rush out to the office,
They do NOT have interminable chats,
They do NOT play Old Maid and Checkers,
They do NOT wear bright yellow spats.

People, of course, will always be people,
     But Cats are Cats.

Dog

Dogs are quite a bit like people,
Or so it seems to me somehow.
Like people, Dogs go anywhere,
They swim in the sea, they leap through the air,
They bark and growl, they sit and stare,
They even wear what people wear.
Look at that Poodle with a hat on its noodle,
Look at that Boxer in a long silver-fox fur,
Look at that Whippet in its calico tippet,
Look at that Sealyham in diamonds from Rotterdam,
Look at that Afghan wrapped in an afghan,
Look at that Chow down there on a dhow
All decked out for some big powwow
With Pekinese waiting to come kowtow.
Don't they all look just like people?
People you've *seen* somewhere? Bowwow!

Fox and Crow

High in the flowering catalpa trees,
Sir Crow in his beak held a large hunk of cheese.
Sir Fox, by its fragrance drawn that way,
Felt himself called upon to say:
"Allow me, Black Majesty, to suggest
That if the wealth of your dark vest
Is matched in fullness by your song,
I cannot think that I am wrong—
You must be a singer beyond compare!"
These words to the Crow were sweet to hear,
And swelling with pride, he flung open his craw,
Emitting a most lugubrious *Caw!*
Down through the branches tumbled the cheese,
Which the Fox gobbled up with the greatest of ease
As he trotted beneath the catalpa trees.

You can swim with a pocket stuffed with rocks
Sooner than you can believe a Fox;
And do *not* try to do what you cannot do
No matter who may want you to!

Cow

Cows are not supposed to fly,
  And so, if you should see
    A spotted Cow go flying by
      Above a pawpaw tree
In a porkpie hat with a green umbrella,
  Then run right down the road and tell a
    Lady selling sarsaparilla,
      Lemon soda and vanilla,
So she can come here and tell me!

Parrot (from Zambezi) _____

A Parrot I bought in Zambezi
Would perch, while I played Parcheesi,
With feathers all ruffled and breezy,
And ask in a voice that was wheezy:
    Boy Blue, is it hot?
      Boy Blue, is it hot?
To that Parrot I bought in Zambezi
That perched, while I played Parcheesi,
With feathers all ruffled and breezy,
I replied—and it was quite easy—
    Certainly not!
      Certainly not!
    Certainly not even half as hot
      As it is
        On the streets of Zambezi!

Gull

Life is seldom if ever dull
For the lazy long-winged white Sea Gull.
    It is as interesting as can be;
He lies on the wind, a slender reed,
And wheels and dips for hours to feed
On scruffy fish and pickleweed
    And to smell the smell of the sea.

He wheels and dips: beneath his wings
The pirate grins, the sailor sings,
    As they ply the China Sea.
While cold winds grip a schooner's sail
And water spouts from a great White Whale,
Perched on a mast, he rides the gale—
    What a wonderful life has he!

Raccoon

One summer night a little Raccoon,
Above his left shoulder, looked at the new moon.
    He made a wish;
    He said: "I wish
    I were a Catfish,
    A Blowfish, a Squid,
    A Katydid,
    A Beetle, a Skink,
    An Ostrich, a pink
    Flamingo, a Gander,
    A Salamander,
    A Hippopotamus,
    A Duck-billed Platypus,
    A Gecko, a Slug,
    A Water Bug,
    A pug-nosed Beaver,
    Anything whatever
Except what I am, a little Raccoon!"

Above his left shoulder, the Evening Star
Listened and heard the little Raccoon
    Who wished on the moon;
    And she said: "Why wish
    You were a Catfish,
    A Blowfish, a Squid,
    A Katydid,
    A Beetle, a Skink,
    An Ostrich, a pink
    Flamingo, a Gander,

A Salamander,
A Hippopotamus,
A Duck-billed Platypus,
A Gecko, a Slug,
A Water Bug,
A pug-nosed Beaver,
Anything whatever?
Why must you change?" said the Evening Star,
"When you are perfect as you are?
I know a boy who wished on the moon
That *he* might be a little Raccoon!"

Polar Bear

I think it must be very nice
To stroll about upon the ice,
Night and day, day and night,
Wearing only black and white,
Always in your Sunday best—
Black tailcoat and pearl-white vest.
To stroll about so pleasantly
Beside the cold and silent sea
Would really suit me to a T!
I think it must be very nice
To stroll with Penguins on the ice.

For those who like the arctic air,
There also is the Polar Bear.

Penguin

The Polar Bear never makes his bed;
He sleeps on a cake of ice instead.
He has no blanket, no quilt, no sheet
Except the rain and snow and sleet.
He drifts about on a white ice floe
While cold winds howl and blizzards blow
And the temperature drops to forty below.
The Polar Bear never makes his bed;
The blanket he pulls up over his head
Is lined with soft and feathery snow.
If ever he rose and turned on the light,
He would find a world of bathtub white,
And icebergs floating through the night.

Giraffe

When I invite the Giraffe to dine,
I ask a carpenter friend of mine
To build a table so very tall
It takes up nearly the whole front hall.
The Giraffe and I do not need chairs:
He stands—I sit on the top of the stairs;
And we eat from crisp white paper plates
A meal of bananas, figs, and dates.

He whispers, when the table's clear,
Just loud enough for me to hear:
"Come one day soon to dine with me
And sit high up in a banyan tree
While Beasts of earth and sea and air
Gather all around us there,
All around the Unicorn
Who leads them with his lowered horn—

And we'll eat *without* white paper plates
A meal of bananas, figs, and dates."

Swan

"You have seen the world, you have seen the zoo,
And the lovely animals," said Boy Blue.
"I am weary now and I long to fly
Round and round in the big blue sky;
And wouldn't you, too, if you were I?"
So he called to the Swan on the edge of the stream,
And the Swan floated up like a ship in a dream,
A ship with billowing sails of white
To take him far into the night.
He climbed on its back, and away they flew.
The children said, "Good-bye! Good-bye!"
"Good-bye to you all!" replied Boy Blue.

THE OLD MAN
FROM OKEFENOKEE:
Loony and Lopsided Limericks

There was an Old Man from Luray
Who always had something to say;
    But each time he tried
    With his mouth opened wide
His big tongue would get in the way.

There was a Young Person named Crockett
Who attached himself to a rocket;
    He flew out through space
    At such a great pace
That his pants flew out of his pocket.

There was an Old Lady named Brown
Who whisked a large fan around town;
    Which might have been good
    Had it not been of wood
And used freely to knock people down.

An Old Man from Okefenokee
Liked to sing in a most dismal low key;
    He would perch on a log
    And boom like a frog
Through the dark swamp of Okefenokee.

There was a Young Lady named Rose
Who was constantly blowing her nose;
    Because of this failing
    They sent her off whaling
So the whalers could say: "Thar she blows!"

There was an Old Lady named Crockett
Who went to put a plug in a socket;
    But her hands were so wet
    She flew up like a jet
And came roaring back down like a rocket!

There was an Old Woman named Piper
Who spoke like a windshield wiper.
    She would say: "Dumb Gump!
    Wet Stump! Wet Stump!"
And then like the voice of disaster
Her words would come faster and faster:
    "Dumb Gump! Dumb Gump!
    Wet Stump! Wet Stump!
    Wet Stump! Wet Stump!
Tiddledy-diddledy-diddledy-bump . . .
    Bump . . .
       Bump . . .
          Bump . . .
            BUMP!"
—Which greatly annoyed *Mr.* Piper!

There was an Old Lady named Hart,
Whose appearance gave people a start:
    Her shape was a candle's,
    Her ears like door handles,
And her front teeth three inches apart.

A Young Man from Old Terre Haute
Had a string of six catfish he'd caught.
   While he lingered to chat,
   They attracted a cat,
Which reduced the six catfish to naught.

A contentious Old Person named Reagan,
Who lived in the heart of Skowhegan,
   Would get in a dither,
   And then on a zither
Play tunes that were dull and fatiguin'.

An obnoxious Old Person named Hackett
Bought a huge trunk and started to pack it.
   When he tripped and fell in it
   And it shut the next minute,
He proceeded to make quite a racket.

THE FLOOR AND

THE CEILING

The Floor and the Ceiling

Winter and summer, whatever the weather,
The Floor and the Ceiling were happy together
In a quaint little house on the outskirts of town
With the Floor looking up and the Ceiling
    looking down.

The Floor bought the Ceiling an ostrich-plumed hat,
And they dined upon drippings of bacon fat,
Diced artichoke hearts and cottage cheese
And hundreds of other such delicacies.

On a screened-in porch in early spring
They would sit at the player piano and sing.
When the Floor cried in French, *"Ah, je vous adore!"*
The Ceiling replied, "You adorable Floor!"

The years went by as the years they will,
And each little thing was fine until
One evening, enjoying their bacon fat,
The Floor and the Ceiling had a terrible spat.

The Ceiling, loftily looking down,
Said, "You are the *lowest* Floor in this town!"
The Floor, looking up with a frightening grin,
Said, "Keep up your chatter, and *you* will cave in!"

So they went off to bed: while the Floor
    settled down,
The Ceiling packed up her gay wallflower gown;
And tiptoeing out past the Chippendale chair
And the gateleg table, down the stair,

Took a coat from the hook and a hat from the rack,
And flew out the door—farewell to the Floor!—
And flew out the door, and was seen no more,
And flew out the door, and *never* came back!

In a quaint little house on the outskirts of town,
Now the shutters go bang, and the walls tumble
  down;
And the roses in summer run wild through the
  room,
But blooming for no one—then why should they
  bloom?

For what is a Floor now that brambles have grown
Over window and woodwork and chimney of stone?
For what is a Floor when the Floor stands alone?
And what is a Ceiling when the Ceiling has flown?

Little Dimity

Poor little pigeon-toed Dimity Drew,
The more she ate, the smaller she grew.
When some people eat, they get taller and taller;
When Dimity ate, she got smaller and smaller.
She went for a walk, and all you could see
Was a tam-o'-shanter the size of a pea,
An umbrella as big as the cross on a *t*,
And a wee pocketbook of butterfly blue.
She came to a crack one half an inch wide,
Tripped on a breadcrumb, fell inside,
And slowly disappeared from view.

Big Gumbo

Great big gawky Gumbo Cole
Couldn't stop growing to save his soul.
Gave up eating, gave up drink,
Sat in the closet, hoped to shrink;
But he grew and grew till he burst the door,
His head went through to the upper floor,
His feet reached down to the cellar door.
He grew still more till the house came down
And Gumbo Cole stepped out on the town
And smashed it in like an old anthill!
Never stopped growing, never will.
Ten times as tall as a telephone pole,
Too big for his breeches—Gumbo Cole!

Banjo Tune

Plunk -a- Plunk! Plunk -a- Plunk!
I sit in the attic on an old trunk.

Plunk -a- Plunk!

Locked in the old trunk is my wife,
And she may be there for the rest of her life.

Plunk -a- Plunk!

She screams, "Let me out of here, you fool!"
I say, "I will when your soup gets cool."

Plunk -a- Plunk!

She screams, "Let me out or I'll bean you, brother!"
I say, "Now, come on, tell me another!"

Plunk -a- Plunk!

To keep one's wife in a trunk is wrong,
But I keep mine there for the sake of my song.

Plunk -a- Plunk!

My song is hokum, my song is bunk,
And there's just a wad of old clothes in this trunk;
Not even the junkman would want this junk!

Plunk -a- Plunk!

Plunk -a- Plunk!

Plunk!

The Crossing of Mary of Scotland

Mary, Mary, Queen of Scots,
Dressed in yellow polka dots,
Sailed one rainy winter day,
Sailed from Dover to Calais,
Sailed in tears, heart tied in knots;
Face broke out in scarlet spots
The size of yellow polka dots—
Forgot to take her *booster* shots,
Queen of Scotland, Queen of Scots!

Mr. Smith

How rewarding to know Mr. Smith,
　　Whose writings at random appear!
Some think him a joy to be with
　　While others do not, it is clear.

His eyes are somewhat Oriental,
　　His fingers are notably long;
His disposition is gentle,
　　He will jump at the sound of a gong.

His chin is quite smooth and uncleft,
　　His face is clean-shaven and bright,
His right arm looks much like his left,
　　His left leg, it goes with his right.

He has friends in the arts and the sciences;
　　He knows only one talent scout;
He can cope with most kitchen appliances,
　　But in general prefers dining out.

When young he collected matchboxes,
　　He now collects notebooks and hats;
He has eaten *roussettes* (flying foxes),
　　Which are really the next thing to bats!

He has never set foot on Majorca,
　　He has been to Tahiti twice
But will seldom, no veteran walker,
　　Take two steps when one will suffice.

He abhors motorbikes and boiled cabbage;
    Zippers he just tolerates;
He is wholly indifferent to cribbage,
    And cuts a poor figure on skates.

He weeps by the side of the ocean,
    And goes back the way that he came;
He calls out his name with emotion—
    It returns to him always the same.

It returns on the wind and he hears it
    While the waves make a rustle around;
The dark settles down, and he fears it.
    He fears its thin, crickety sound.

He thinks more and more as time passes,
    Rarely opens a volume on myth.
Until mourned by the tall prairie grasses,
    How rewarding to know Mr. Smith!

The King of Spain

"I like this book," said the King of Spain.
"I think I'll read it through again."

The Author

WILLIAM JAY SMITH, the distinguished poet, is the author of *The Traveler's Tree: New and Selected Poems* and of *Army Brat, a Memoir,* which tells about his growing up as the son of an enlisted man in the regular Army. Mr. Smith has written a number of books of poetry for children and has edited, with Louise Bogan, the well-known anthology *The Golden Journey.* His nonsense poems have appeared in anthologies throughout the English-speaking world.

The Artist

FERNANDO KRAHN, artist, cartoonist, and film-maker, is the creator of many imaginative picture books for children, including *How Santa Claus Had a Long and Difficult Journey Delivering His Presents, Journeys of Sebastian, Sebastian and the Mushroom,* and *Hildegarde and Maxmilian.*

811
Sm   Smith, William Jay

            Laughing time

DATE DUE

DEC 21	3t	
JAN 19		
3F	3S	
JUN 11	OCT 2 9 1987	
NOV 10	3 S	
DEC 1	5s	
Ke	2B	
JAN 1 3	APR 5 '91	
Bain	'JAN 9 1992	
JUN 10	FEB 22 '93	
Boiled	2B	
MAY 3 1984	Fischer